The Last Covenant

Choral Readings
For Good Friday
And Easter Day

Lynda Pujadó

CSS Publishing Company, Inc.
Lima, Ohio

THE LAST COVENANT

ISBN 0-7880-0226-0

PRINTED IN U.S.A.

To God's Glory
and
Heidi
Inga
Marlys

Table Of Contents

Notes

Both choral readings, "The Last Covenant" and "Sent To Calvary," are intended for five voices. Any type and combination of voices — male or female — would be appropriate and effective. A melodious combination of voices will convey the strong emotions and word pictures of the drama of the death and resurrection of Christ.

The readings could be performed as choir litanies, with the ALL parts being read by the congregation. No memorization, costumes or props are necessary.

The
Last
Covenant

Worship Service

Call To Worship
L: Blessed is our Lord and Savior, Jesus Christ.
C: **We long for his presence. We seek his will above our own. Our hope is his eternal word.**

L: Our God is holy, now and forever. Praise to our Lord!
C: **He made us. He knows us. He hears our prayers and answers us. He calls us to holiness. He calls us to himself.**

L: Jesus is compassionate, patient, understanding and forgiving.
C: **He wants our hearts with his. He plans good things for us. He teaches us to live in this world, but for eternal values.**

L: Jesus loves us. He died for us. He lives forever.
C: **There is no depth our Savior cannot reach to keep us close to him. He is everything to us. We want the value of our lives to mirror the value of the Resurrection. Glory be to God and our Savior, Jesus Christ!**

Psalm 22:1-5

Second Scripture Lesson: Romans 6:4-6

Prayer Of The Church
Dear Heavenly Father,
You have done everything for us so we may come to you now and forever. You have given us your son, Jesus Christ, our Lord, Friend, and Savior who lives with us, knows us, suffers with us and guides us into eternity.

There is no depth he has not or will not fathom on our behalf. Help us to bring the Resurrection and Heaven's reality to others by being compassionate and concerned, and by supplying individual needs selflessly to others the way you do to us.

Allow us to live fully the gift and mystery of faith which you desire for each of us and to live a close, personal, daily relationship with you which proves your presence and active involvement in our lives.

Let us claim your Easter peace to live in, and your wisdom to solve earthly problems, using eternal values.

In the name of Jesus, Amen.

The Last Covenant

Voice

1   For about three years, Jesus had been with his friends, the disciples.

4,5   They were constantly together.

2,3   Jesus had called them.

2,5   His voice had the power of eternity in it and —

4   It was definite when you heard your name being called by Christ.

3   It was not only a man that called you,

2,3,4 But God,

1,5   Eternity

ALL And truth.

Hymn: "All Glory Laud And Honor" (vv. 1 and 2)

3   Jesus represented a truth to his friends that they could not comprehend and were always trying to understand.

2,4   It was not easy to understand Christ.

1,2,3 He explained God to them and his kingdom of eternity.

3,5   They did not understand, because he often spoke in spiritual terms.

ALL God is Spirit.

5   Multitudes were attracted to him because of the depth and power of his voice, and the miracles that they could not deny.

1,4   He introduced love for other people and he proved it.

2,3,5   Again and again.

3,4   People loved him for his kindness and for the power of his teaching.

1,3,5   The popularity of Christ spread among all classes of people.

1,2   His popularity was poison to the Pharisees.

4,5   And they became embittered with the carpenter's son.

1,4   Jealous.

2,3   Hostile.

2,5   Angry.

Hymn: "On My Head Imprint Your Image"

2   They could not understand his concept of love which always transgressed their religious laws.

3,4   After all, they had God under their control.

1,5   God did not belong to anyone else.

2,3,4   They used him for their own benefit.

2,5   Christ introduced God to everyone by what he said and did.

3,4 Many people believed he was the son of God —

ALL That was his problem.

1,2 This was not convenient for the Pharisees.

4,5 And then it happened.

ALL Gradually.

1,4 But definitely.

2,3 They wanted him condemned.

2,5 They were evil and wicked in intent.

1,3,4 They approached Judas as an accomplice.

3,5 It was an easy task, and nothing important, they explained to him.

1,2,4 He knew Christ well, but more importantly —

5 He loved money.

2,3 It was a disease that held him prisoner and which he thrived on,

1,5 As the Pharisees thrived on their hatred of Christ.

ALL And, they loved their cruelty.

Hymn: "Glory Be To Jesus" (v. 1)

2 At the Passover celebration, Jesus had taken bread, given thanks and gave it to Judas and the others.

4 He said, "This is my body which is given for you. Do this in remembrance of me."[1]

1,2,5 He also took a cup of wine and gave it to them.

3,4 He said it was his blood poured out and a new covenant in his blood.

ALL They did not understand.

4,5 There had been many covenants between God and his people.

1 God promised Abraham and his descendants blessings through faith in the first covenant between God and his people.

2,3 God gave Moses the law and legal codes on Mount Sinai.

1,2,4 God repeated many promises in his covenant with David.

5 In the Jeremiah Covenant, God put his laws in the hearts of his people.

1,4 God gave covenants to Ezekiel and to Isaiah for his people.

3 And now, during Passover, Jesus Christ, the Son of God, promised another covenant with those who believed in him.

ALL It was a covenant in his blood.

3,5 Poured out, he said to the disciples as they sat in the upper room.

1,2,4 It would be a human sacrifice for the forgiveness of sins.

2,5 But no one understood what he meant. The topic was left undiscussed.

1   Then Judas got up and left the group.

2,4,5 They went into the Garden of Gethsemane, which was often their custom.

1,3   Judas was not with them, but he knew about the garden.

2,5   He had been there before.

3   And he knew Christ would be there.

1,4   All Judas had to do was give a sign to the Pharisees.

4,5   He would give a definite sign to them, but nothing unusual.

1,2,3 Certainly, it would be easily done.

1,5   Judas could collect his money and everything would be the same.

2,4   He would still be a disciple and follow Christ as usual, he supposed.

3,4,5 He was one of the twelve, absolutely.

1,3   Quickly, the Pharisees followed Judas, the friend of Christ.

2   Judas was only doing the Pharisees a favor, he said to himself as he kissed the man in the darkness.

4   He felt comfortable in the night, as though he belonged there, and well hidden from the light of day.

Hymn: "Ah, Holy Jesus" (v. 1)

1   Soon, there were hundreds of thundering soldiers, marching in the garden, and they surrounded the man of prayer.

3   In the quietness of the night, their golden torch flames screamed gaily as they shone on the face of a man betrayed by a friend —

4,5   And the terror pierced the disciples' hearts.

1,2,3   Many disciples ran away from the soldiers of death, not knowing where to go.

2,4   Leaving their Master, the disciples had nothing.

5   As they fled, they saw not only the sharp, piercing spears of brutal cruelty, but the impossible kiss of Judas, easily given.

1,2   It was innocently done as a man to his friend —

3,5   Or son to his father.

1,2,4   Had not Judas been one of them?

2,3   He had followed Christ and known his deeds.

3,4   Judas had listened to his voice!

1,5   Now, they did not understand this man.

2   But worse, they did not understand themselves because they could not be criminals of the state and they could not be in this intolerable situation.

4,5   They had only followed Christ, the man who was God and truth.

1,2,4   However, they had never associated truth with suffering or personal hardship.

2,3,5   Now, following the man of truth and eternity meant paying a high premium.

1,3 It could not be true that Christ would allow the nightmare which confronted them.

3,4 The nightmare encompassed them, their brains and thinking powers.

2,5 It tore at their hearts and inside fiber of being.

1 They were surrounded in an impossible, incomprehensible, living horror while the golden, searing flames of the night's torches kept dancing wildly and the horror grew worse.

2 Their Master disappeared into the consuming night's blackness and he stood alone encircled by jealous, evil men.

Hymn: "In The Hour Of Trial" (vv. 1 and 2)

1,4 Behind closed doors, they took him without witnesses or friends.

3,5 The Pharisees held their trials in illegal secrecy.

2,3,4 They, like Judas, found the night to be their friend.

4 In paralyzing fear, Peter followed Christ, and after denying him for the third time, sobs vibrated throughout his body. His remorse and guilt were unbelievable.

1,5 There was nothing he or the others could hang onto now.

3 When Christ was taken to Pilate early Friday morning, the disciples felt a nauseating, frightening sickness.

2,4 The Jews condemned him for being the son of God and a traitor.

1,3 Pilate found him innocent, but wondered if he might be an evil spirit and feared him.

5 Pilate's wife begged him to leave him alone. God had talked to her in a dream, and Pilate again feared Christ.

3,4 Christ was sent to Herod Antipas for closer investigation.

1,2 Herod wanted to be entertained by the man of miracles as he assumed so many other people had been.

2,3,5 The prisoner remained silent and immobile.

1,4 Herod wondered if the man might really be the spirit of John the Baptist whom he had recently murdered.

2,5 Herod declared the man guilty. Besides, he was boring and useless to him.

1,3,4 Pilate conveniently exchanged him for Barabbas, the murderer, although personally he did not consider him guilty.

1 For political reasons, it would be better for Pilate to have Christ crucified. The Jews would be appeased and so would the Caesar who gave him his job.

4 Hideously wicked, ecstatic screams rose from the Pharisees when Pilate washed his hands in front of them and the bound prisoner stood beaten and condemned before them.

2,3 Since Jesus was too weak to carry the wooden timbers to die on, a stranger was pulled out from the Passover crowd.

ALL The disciples knew his name.

5   Raging with guilt, they all knew well that Simon from Cyrene in Africa, and not one of them, was carrying their Master's cross.

1,4   Not one of them was near their Master now because they feared that his death might be contagious to them.

ALL   It was happening so fast.

3   Few who knew the man from Nazareth were aware of his sudden condemnation. Criminals were crucified frequently and besides, this man was well loved.

1,2,4   No one would consider him a man to be crucified.

5   And people went on with their daily affairs, oblivious to the painfully faltering, swaggering steps of the carpenter's son whom they loved.

2,3   So many had loved him.

3,4,5   Thousands.

1   But few were at the place of the skull to see the man of God publicly exhibited in torture.

2,5   Mary was there. She was his mother.

Hymn: "At The Cross Her Station Keeping" (vv. 1 and 2)

1,4   Mary had known him all his life.

1,2,3   She saw him nailed and lifted up.

3,5   John was there and saw his Master gasp in suffocating agony.

1,4   Christ had been betrayed by a friend.

19

4	He was taunted and jeered at by men who did not know him and who found his crucifixion a casual social event and a source of entertainment.
2,3	His body screamed with searing, shocking pain.
1,5	His limbs were pulled out of their sockets.
1,2,4	The blood could not circulate and he could not breathe.
1,3	His mind was threatened with insanity because of the intolerable pain.
2,5	Jesus forgave his enemies, gave up his spirit and died.
3,4	He died in overwhelming loneliness and bitter humiliation.
1,3,5	His friends were numbed with deepening pain.
ALL	It was real.
2,4,5	Christ had suffered and died.
1,3	Excruciating mental confusion confronted his followers.
2	Their minds and lives had been tortured, fragmented and ruined, just as though they had been Christ.
4,5	They could not think of what had happened.
2,3	They had nowhere to go.
1,5	They did not know what to do.
4,2	There was no purpose in living. There would be no eternal kingdom.

Hymn: "When I Survey The Wondrous Cross" (v. 1)

1 As soon as it was legally possible, on the third day the women went to the tomb to anoint the body.

3,4,5 They went knowing it was impossible for them to enter.

4 There were strong, well paid Roman soldiers guarding the tomb and the Pharisees had a stone angled in so no one could remove it.

1,2,3 It was dangerous for the women. They were not wanted there.

3 They had no way to defend themselves against the soldiers who could harm them or treat them with contempt.

1,5 The Pharisees were correct in thinking that no one could remove the mighty rock in front of the grave's entrance.

ALL Only God could.

2,4 In the early morning, God sent an angel to remove the barrier.

3 As the women came close to the tomb, they saw the soldiers lying still and mute, as though they were brainless or dormant.

1 They had been paralyzed with unspeakable fear from the angel's activities.

1,2,5 The women entered the tomb to find only neatly rolled bandages and Christ was gone.

3,4 More despair and deeper feelings of hopelessness entered their hearts.

1,5 They asked the man in the garden where the Christ was.

2,4 He answered them quietly.

1,2,5 He had been waiting for them.

1,3,4 At first, the women did not recognize the man in the garden.

3,5 He was a man who had been beaten beyond recognition and crucified.

1,2 But they recognized his power of compassion and they knew him.

5 With increasing wonder and awe, they realized that the man was their Savior. Into their crushed and buried lives, abundant, joyful life flowed slowly back into them.

2 It was impossible that he was alive, but they recalled his words about his suffering and dying.

ALL His kingdom was forever, now.

3,4 Christ had proved that eternity with him exists for those that believe in him.

Hymn: "Praise The Savior" (v. 1)

1,2,5 The women went to tell the others.

3,4 They went to explain that Christ was alive and no longer in the tomb!

3,4,5 God's son was alive. He was the last sacrifice.

2,5 His blood was poured out for our sins and for eternal life.

1,3 His covenant is forever.

3   There was rejoicing among his friends and their love and devotion grew strong and dedicated to eternity.

1,4   Suffering and death arc a reality, but Christ's kingdom is eternal.

ALL Alleluia!

5   Christ loves us! There is eternal hope for everyone!

ALL Alleluia!

2,3   Believe in Christ and live with him forever!

ALL Alleluia!

ALL Amen!

Hymn: "Jesus Christ Is Risen Today" (vv. 1 and 4)

The End

Scripture Quote
1. Luke 22:19b

Sent
To
Calvary

Sent To Calvary

Voice

1   The carpenter's son, Jesus of Nazareth born in Bethlehem, was with his disciples Thursday night.

ALL   They gathered to celebrate the Passover Feast together.

3,4   They gathered as friends with their Lord and Savior.

2   Jesus gave thanks to God and took a cup of wine and then passed it among his friends.

5   Jesus gave thanks to God and took bread, broke it and gave it to them.

1,2   He said, "This is my body which is given for you. Do this in remembrance of me."[1]

3,4   He said, "... this is my blood of the covenant, which is poured out for many for the forgiveness of sins."[2]

5   Jesus then said one of them would betray him.

ALL   One would betray him.

1   One of the twelve.

ALL   And they looked around the room among themselves, wondering.

4   They went out in the night to the Garden of Gethsemane where Jesus often prayed.

1,5   He had taught them how to pray himself.

2   They had wanted to. They wanted to be like Christ.

3   Jesus was a man of deep prayer.

5   Now, in the Garden, Jesus prayed long into the night.

ALL Soon, there was a multitude of footsteps coming.

1   Lighted torches gleamed brazenly in the quiet garden of prayer.

2   Footsteps and voices of men who were companions of brutal death.

3,4 Footsteps coming faster — heavy footsteps of armed soldiers.

5   To the terrified disciples, the universe became still, almost as though the moon and stars were in anguish, wondering whether they too would be disrupted and, like Christ, be jarred out of place.

1   Jesus, with humility and compassion, confronted the trained warriors.

ALL A silent kiss brushed his cheek.

2   "Friend," Judas said to the man in the Garden. They had been friends.

2,3 Silent screams rose up from the disciples. Terrifying screams.

1,5 The eyes and power of Christ shocked the soldiers.

2   They fell back from Christ and his power of eternity.

3,4 "Why didn't you come for me during the day?" Christ said to them.

5   But they were paid to be men of the night.

1   The night was a friend to Satan and Judas.

2   The night was a friend to the Pharisees and chief priests.

3   The darkness hid them. It hid their deeds from the light of day.

4   It was convenient to steal Jesus away from prayer with God Almighty.

ALL Alone, Jesus faced his trials with no witnesses.

5   Alone, he was mocked, beaten and taunted.

1,2 The Pharisees did their work at night.

ALL "Are you the Son of God?" they asked him with blazing eyes.

3,4 "Are you the Son of God?" they said with bitterness and anger.

5   "Yes," the carpenter's son answered.

1   In ecstasy, the Jews handed him over to Pilate. It was a clear case. He rivaled the state authorities with importance. He also blasphemed.

ALL Yet, Friday morning, after the secret trials and severe beatings, Pilate could find no guilt in him, nor Herod either.

2   In an angry, jealous mob, the Pharisees called out, "Crucify him!"

3   Pilate was firm. The man was innocent.

4,5   Like tumultuous ocean waves in a storm, the raging insistence of the mob increased.

1,2   Pilate saw them as a political enemy — a massive enemy complaining to Caesar. And Pilate worried about losing his job.

3,4   He couldn't afford to lose his job just because of a strange man claiming to be God's son.

5   And his wife came to him, pleading with him about the voice of God telling her not to have anything to do with Jesus the Christ.

1   Pilate couldn't deny the powerful calmness about Jesus or the depth of honesty in his answers.

2,3   The mob's anger swelled and Pilate could see himself soon as a victim of their wrath.

ALL   Christ was innocent. Pilate said so again and again. It was certain.

4,5   They engulfed him with their irrational fury, igniting him, like flames from a fire out of control.

5   He compromised truth which cannot be compromised and exchanged Barabbas for the Christ. Barabbas, a man of murder and feared by society.

1,2   Pilate sent the man of peace, the man who spoke with such a depth of integrity that it was hard to understand him, to a death of horrors.

3   And the carpenter's son, born of Mary and placed in a stable, the carpenter's son, whom the angels proclaimed to the shepherds in Bethlehem, was sent to Calvary because he said he was God's son.

4,5 As preparation for the crucifixion, Jesus of Nazareth was beaten and scourged beyond recognition, even though Pilate said he was innocent.

1,2 The man was nailed to a cross and hoisted up while Pilate breathed easily because his job remained safe. He would be a popular man again.

3 Some friends of Jesus came to Calvary to see the unbelievable nightmare which was taking place. But fear scattered most disciples. If Roman soldiers could come for the Son of God in the Garden of Gethsemane, they could easily come for any of them.

ALL Fear and confusion spread through the followers.

4,5 Confusion and pain.

1 Who could help them? Where could they go?

2 They had not needed help before. Jesus helped others. He did not require help himself. The disciples had always come to him for help.

3,4 Why didn't Jesus do something? He could do something!

ALL He had always done miracles.

5 The water turned into wine at the wedding in Cana. His first miracle.

1,2 The blind man at the Pool of Siloam who was made to see.

ALL There were so many miracles.

3 Mary came to Golgotha. She was his mother. He was beloved to her.

4 John came.

5   Martha and her sister Mary came. They also loved Jesus.

1,2   In excruciating pain, Jesus was suffocating to death.

3   While Jesus was asking God to forgive his enemies, the soldiers cast lots for his clothes. They were used to death. It was their business.

4,5   Darkness covered the earth when Jesus was on the cross. There was an earthquake, a shaking of the earth as if God's hands were shaking his beloved world to realize his son was dying.

ALL "My God, My God, why have you forsaken me?" Jesus said on the cross.[3]

5   The centurion noticed him dying, yet speaking profoundly with God.

1,2   Jesus cried, "Father, into your hands I commend my spirit," and he died.[4] The centurion heard him. His voice was from God. He saw him die and believed he was the son of God.

2   There would be no more sacrifices. Jesus died for our sins.

3   The Pharisees took Jesus very seriously. They remembered what he had said about rising after three days. They had his tomb sealed and guarded.

4,5   The disciples were so consumed with fear that they couldn't think straight. They worried they would be crucified next.

1   The women went to anoint the body early Sunday morning.

4   They worried that the gravestone would be too difficult for them to move. It was a large stone. The Pharisees wanted it that way.

5   Before they arrived, an angel of the Lord moved the stone.

1,2   The soldiers felt the earth move underneath them. They fell down in paralyzing terror at seeing the stone move.

3   They appeared to be asleep when the women came to the tomb.

4,5   Carefully, the women entered the dark tomb.

ALL   The linen wrappings of Christ's body were found neatly folded in place, but there was no body.

1   Deeply hurt and their memories flooded with emotional trauma from the crucifixion, they didn't know where to go.

1,3   The Gardener said to Mary, "Why are you crying?"

4,5   She heard the voice. It was the voice of her master.

1   She saw eternity in his eyes and knew her Savior was alive.

ALL   Jesus was alive!

2   The women were filled with joy that overcame the deepest horrors of the crucifixion.

ALL   He came back to them.

3   The Pharisees would have to deal with the disappearance of Christ's body and the people that reported seeing him alive.

4   They would have to do something else, say something to cover up.

5   They could not crucify him again.

1,2   Intense exaltation radiated among the friends of Christ.

3,4   Their spirits rose to Heaven!

5   Christ conquered death.

ALL There is no fear in death now!

1,2   Eternal life reigns for all who believe in Jesus of Nazareth.

3,4   Alleluia!

5   Alleluia!

ALL Amen!

The End

Scripture Quotes
1. Luke 22:19
2. Matthew 26:28
3. Matthew 27:46
4. Luke 23:46

www.ingramcontent.com/pod-product-compliance
Lightning Source LLC
Chambersburg PA
CBHW071802020426
42331CB00008B/2374